TECH SMARTS

12 QUESTIONS ABOUT ONLINE IDENTITY AND PRIVACY

BLACK RABBIT BOOKS | MARYSA STORM

Table of Contents

A nice person could act
a different way online.

What Is an *Online Identity?*

1

Your **identity** is unique to you. It is made of your likes, dislikes, and personality. It is who you are and where you come from. Your class, gender, and beliefs are also included. All these make up your real identity. This is who you are as a person. Your online identity is similar. It is who you are online. But this identity isn't usually complete. And you might not know what's all included.

When you **browse** online, websites learn a little about you. They create blocks of information. These are used to create your online identity. Each site only sees a small part of you. It creates a **partial** identity. Let's say you order a new sweater online. The site stores this information. It may remember next time. Your sweater size is part of your identity. Sites may collect the information and use it. You might not know when a site creates a partial identity for you.

A **persona** is an identity you create. When you make a post, you develop your persona. You decide what is part of it. It may not be the same as your real identity.

THINK ABOUT IT

Make a list of the partial identities you think you have. How are they similar to parts of your real identity? How are they different?

2 Can My Online Identity Differ from *My Real One?*

Each person describes themselves differently. Some people say they are cheerful. Others may say they are outgoing. These are characteristics. They describe how people relate to others. You interact with parents, teachers, and friends. This can help you decide how to describe yourself.

Imagine a girl describes herself as shy. She doesn't often speak up in class. She would rather read than meet new people. Now imagine she is chatting with an online friend. They joke and chat often. That friend probably wouldn't know the girl is shy.

It doesn't matter if it's real life or online. It's always important to be yourself. But online, it's easier to choose how much you share. Some people only show certain parts of their personalities. A shy person may

gh! my mom took my pho
sigh im b
I DONT WANN
THIS IS THE W
....
my head
im so
BAD HA
i have no
IM
im
IM T

be more outgoing online. People have the chance to be a little different online.

Online interactions are different from personal ones. You don't often get to hear others' voices. You don't see gestures or expressions. It can be hard to understand what another person thinks. They might not show how they are truly feeling.

People often spend hours online each day.

GEORGE HERBERT MEAD George Herbert Mead was a scientist. He lived during the late 1800s and early 1900s. He studied people's minds and behaviors. According to his work, personalities are shaped by time spent with others. The way you think about yourself reflects what others think of you.

3 How Do I Protect My *Private Information?*

Many websites gather your personal information. They do this to sell you products. On some sites you need an account. Some of the info a site asks for is optional. You decide whether you give it out. It is best to limit what you share when you can.

There are two basic kinds of information. The first is personal information. This includes facts about you. It could be your favorite food or subject. It cannot be used to identify you. Private information can identify you. This is the second kind of information. It includes your address and phone number.

Personal information is safer to share than private. But it can be easy for private information to slip out. You might share that you love the pizza your school serves.

This is personal information. But the name of your school is private. And you could share that by accident.

Sharing information is risky. If you share too much, someone could steal your identity. This is **identity theft**. Thieves steal other people's Social Security numbers. They take their birth dates or credit card numbers. They use the **data** to get identification cards or credit cards. Identity thieves are hard to catch. Many of them do not care how they hurt real people.

Your social security number is how the government identifies you.

30 Percent of Americans who have been a victim of identity theft.

Americans can report identity theft to the Federal Trade Commission (FTC). • Reports of identity theft are on the rise. • The FTC received more than 1 million reports in 2023.

Victims can lose thousands of dollars to identity theft.

When Is My Personal Information *Collected Online?*

4

On many sites, you create an account. As you do so, you agree to the sites' terms and conditions. This gives the site permission to collect your data. It is unlikely a company will contact you directly. But once you give information away, there is often no way to get it back. You may not even be able to ask a company to remove it. You can delete your account. But the site will still have your data.

Companies use parts of your identity to make money. They create targeted advertisements, or ads. These are specific to your interests. Sites track your online activity. They might use data from sites you visit and online purchases. You can decide whether to give companies this data.

Most Americans are surprised by the amount of information companies collect. Some people want to be able to control how much information they provide. This is especially important for parents. They want to protect

Make sure to keep your personal details private.

12 Maximum age of the children COPPA protects.

Many kids don't understand how businesses collect and use info. COPPA helps protect them. • COPPA gives parents the power to decide what info is shared about their kids. • Mobile games and other apps may not follow COPPA rules.

their kids. In 1998, Congress passed a new law. It was called the Children's Online Privacy Protection Act (COPPA). It limits the information sites may collect from kids. It helps protect their online privacy.

Kids have more protections than adults for online security.

SHARE WITH CARE You can limit how much information sites collect about you. One way is to be mindful of what you share online. Keep your location private. Think before you post pictures of yourself. Is your school's logo in the photo? Can someone find out where you are? If yes, then do not post it. Blur or crop out this information. If you are unsure, ask a trusted adult.

How Do Web Browsers *Use Cookies?*

5

Your web browser stores a cookie from each website you visit. A cookie is a strand of information. It is made up of little bits of data you leave behind. Sites save cookies in your browser. When you go back to the site, the cookies remember you. This is how your **preferences** are saved. The cookie remembers what you like. It makes it easier to use the site.

A different kind of cookie tracks what you do online. It is called a third-party cookie. Third-party cookies share your information with advertisers. They use the info to show you targeted ads.

You can delete cookies from your browser. An adult can show you how. But some sites will not work without them. If you don't agree to cookies, you can't go on the site. When you first reach a site, there's often a pop-up. It gives you the choice to reject or accept cookies. You can choose to only allow necessary cookies. These are cookies the site needs to work correctly. They do not include third-party cookies. But you should still be mindful of what you share.

Website pop-ups are called adware.

Websites have to warn you if they collect cookies.

42.2 Percent of websites that use cookies.

Site cookies can remember log-in information. • Third-party cookies are also known as tracking cookies. • Session cookies are temporary. They go away when you close your browser.

Warning

This website uses cookies

Reject Accept

Phone passwords protect your apps, pictures, and videos from other people.

Why Should I Change *My Passwords?*

6

Every account you make needs a password. Passwords help **secure** your information. Strong passwords can protect your online identity. They keep your information safe from other users.

Many people use the same password everywhere. Others may use similar passwords. But experts say to use a different password for each account. Hackers can easily figure out common passwords. This is because many include personal information. People often use birthdays or the name of a pet. This information can be easy to find out.

Most passwords are at least eight **characters**. But longer is always better. A secure password is long, random, and unique. You should use both lowercase and uppercase letters. Include numbers and symbols too. This will make it harder to guess.

Memorize your passwords. Never keep them written down, especially near the computer. Instead, use a password manager. This is a site that keeps track of passwords. It is secure. Only share your passwords with a trusted adult. Do not give them to your friends. And definitely don't give them to people you meet online. Protecting your passwords helps protect your online identity.

A secure password keeps your accounts safe from hackers.

Random characters are better for a password than full words.

127 Maximum number of characters a Microsoft password can contain.

Use a different password for each online account. • Change your password every three months. • Replacing letters with numbers can help make strong passwords.

What Dangers Should I Look Out *for Online?*

7 You can find all sorts of information online. But some content is not appropriate for young people. Few laws control what is put on the internet. It is easy to make a website. Anyone can build one to show anything.

Some sites sell stolen and illegal goods. This is illegal. But creating the website to show the items is not. There are also sites that support harmful things, such as drug use. An internet search can lead you to **offensive** material. It is important to know what you are looking for online. Having a plan can help you avoid bad content.

It is especially important to be careful when chatting online. Chats make communication easier. But it's hard to know whom you're talking to. It is common for adult **predators** to use chat. They pretend to be

500,000 Estimated number of predators online each day.

The FBI investigates online predators. • There are few laws **regulating** the internet. • If someone makes you uncomfortable, block them. Do not reply.

Some sites support the use of illegal substances.

children or teens. They talk about normal things, such as movies. Eventually, they earn a child's trust. They may ask to meet face to face. This would put the child in danger.

It can be difficult to know if you are talking to a predator. Watch for signs. They may ask personal questions. They might ask you to send pictures. If you feel uncomfortable, tell an adult. Do not video chat with someone you do not know in real life. Stay alert. Trust your gut. It's all part of being smart online.

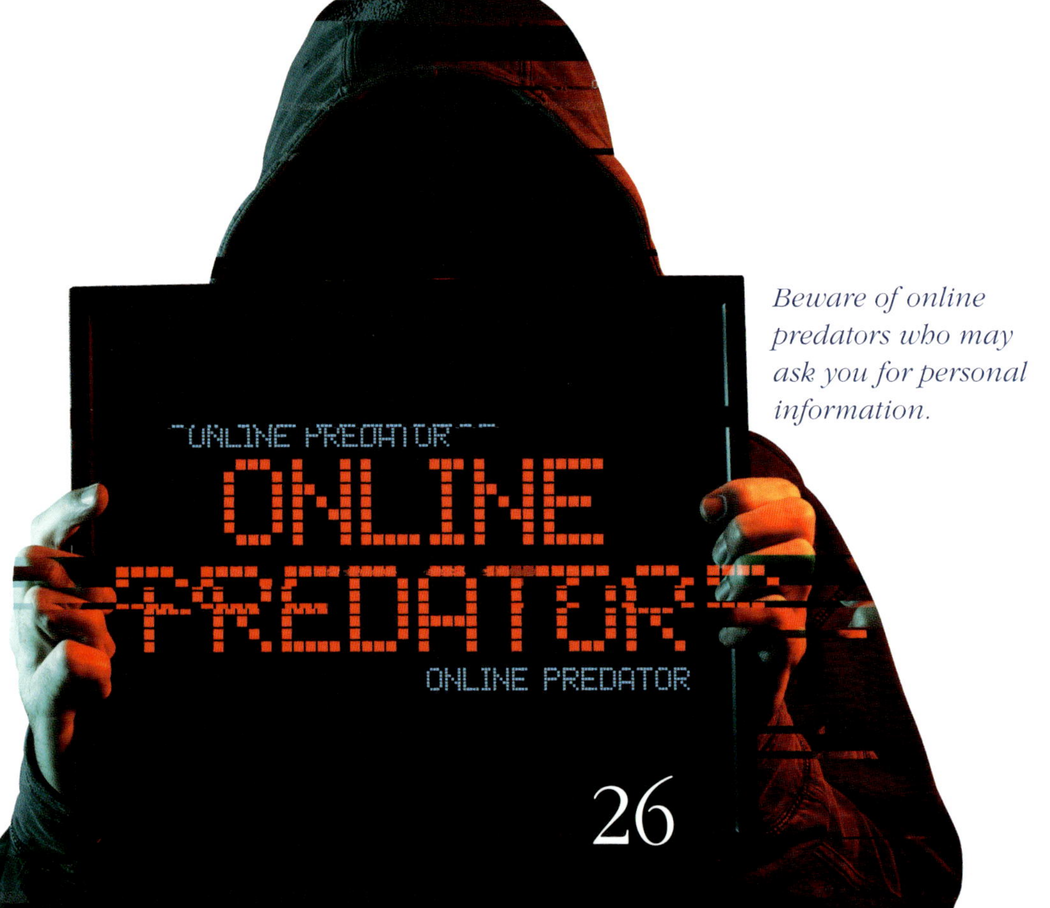

Beware of online predators who may ask you for personal information.

Why Do My Parents Care *What I Do Online?*

8

It might feel like adults watch your online activity too much. They might ask questions about what you do online. They might ask for your passwords. It can feel like they are invading your privacy. Most of the time, that is not the case. Trusted adults look out for your safety. They want to help protect you.

Parents might ask that you only go online at certain times. They might check your search history. This way, they can **monitor** your activity. They want to know that you use the internet responsibly. This helps them trust your judgment. You can explore the internet together. You can also share your interests.

Are you curious about a weird site? It is okay to ask questions. This helps you learn to use the internet responsibly. It can also help start important conversations

Parents can use passwords and other tools to limit their child's access to harmful content.

about staying safe. Try talking with a parent. Ask a teacher. Learning about online dangers now will help keep you safe. You can keep an eye out for anything that feels off.

13 Age most adults think children should be before using the internet on their own.

Your parents and school might block certain sites. • Keep your accounts set to private. This can keep you safe. • Experts say communicating with trusted adults is key to staying safe online.

Can I Delete Things I Write and *Upload Online?*

9

The information you put online builds your online identity. So does the content others post about you. But sometimes, you might post something you regret. Someone else could post stuff about you that you don't like.

You can usually hide what you put on social media or another site. But it is never truly gone. Look through a site's comment section. You might see a post that says, "deleted comment." The words are no longer there. But the spot for that comment still exists. With a little work, people can still get that information. Most people will not try to do this. But some might. Some people might screenshot your posts. This means they will have a copy even if you delete it.

Deleting content is the best way to remove small mistakes. But sometimes you need to delete something more private. You can contact the site's owner and ask them for help. The owner helps the site run smoothly. They also control the site's content. They can decide whether to remove unwanted material. If someone shares something offensive, you can report the post.

Mistakes happen. But the internet is not very forgiving. It can be tricky to undo something. Think carefully before you share content.

Online mistakes are hard to erase.

70 Percent of teens who hid their online activity from their parents in 2024.

This increased from 45 percent in 2010. • Around 50 percent of teens clear their browsing history regularly. • Teens often hide violent content.

THINK ABOUT IT Have you ever wished you could take back something you put online? What did you do when it happened? Make a list of the steps you could take if it happened again.

Everything you post online becomes part of your digital footprint.

What Are *Supercookies?*

10

People worry about their online privacy. They feel like they have less now than in the past. People want their privacy protected. Some may demand sites protect their information. If not, they may take their business elsewhere. Sites will want to protect their customers.

As sites add more privacy controls, trackers create stronger cookies. Some sites now use supercookies. These are permanently stored on a user's computer. You can turn off normal cookies. This is done by selecting the "Do Not Track" option in your browser. But supercookies bypass this setting. They continue to track your online movement. They still work even if your browser is set to private. Even ad blockers can't stop them.

Experts say the public's desire for privacy will eventually win over supercookies. Some browsers

29 Number of months Verizon used supercookies without customer choice.
This occurred from December 2012 to March 2015. • Verizon paid a fine of $1,350,000 for this activity. • About half of Americans don't know what cookies are. • Firefox blocked supercookies from tracking across sites in 2021.

are already blocking third-party cookies. But no one can really see into the future. The best way to protect your privacy tomorrow is to look out for it today.

PRIVACY

What Can I Do to Protect *Myself Online?*

11

Staying safe online keeps you safe in real life. Secure your accounts with strong passwords. Some sites have security questions too. Remember to share this information only with a trusted adult. If you've shared it with others, make sure to update your passwords. Sometimes, that might not be enough. You may need to delete your account. You can also contact a website's owner. They can shut down your account for you. Then you can open a new one.

Whenever you create a new account, check out the privacy settings. They let you control who can see what you share. Be smart about what you post. The best way to protect your identity is to not share private or personal information. Think twice before you post. Do not share when you go on vacation. Thieves often look on social media to learn when families will be out of town.

Have you ever heard the saying "the internet is forever?" Nothing truly gets deleted online. If you would not want a grandparent to read your post, do not share it.

Antivirus programs can help stop a hacker attack.

SPYWARE

mSpy is a **spyware** application for devices. It monitors texts and calls. It sees social media chats. It even tracks the physical location of the device. You cannot tell if mSpy is used on your device. Parents use it to monitor their children. Employers also use it to watch their employees.

34 Percent of Americans who say they update their passwords regularly.

Take time to review your friends and followers online. • Remove any followers you don't recognize. • Protect yourself and your device by avoiding pop-up ads. • Don't click on anything strange.

How Can My Online Identity *Help Me?*

12

Your online identity can be helpful. So can the way you use the internet. Over time, your online identity could shape who you are in real life. A healthy curiosity online can help you discover more in real life.

Using the web safely will help build a positive online identity. Having positive online interactions with others can do this too. It's important to have a good online presence. Someday you will apply for jobs. You might send out college applications. People there will look at your online presence. Try doing an internet search for your name. Does anything come up? If so, are they a good reflection of who you are?

When you use the internet safely, you can learn lots of new things. You can then share what you have learned. This creates a positive online identity. Instead of sharing private information, you are sharing knowledge. You can take this knowledge with you in real life. It helps make you who you are.

The internet is part of almost everything we do today. Being a smart user will help you control your privacy. If used correctly, it can help shape your identity in positive ways. Be mindful about your online activity. It can greatly impact your future.

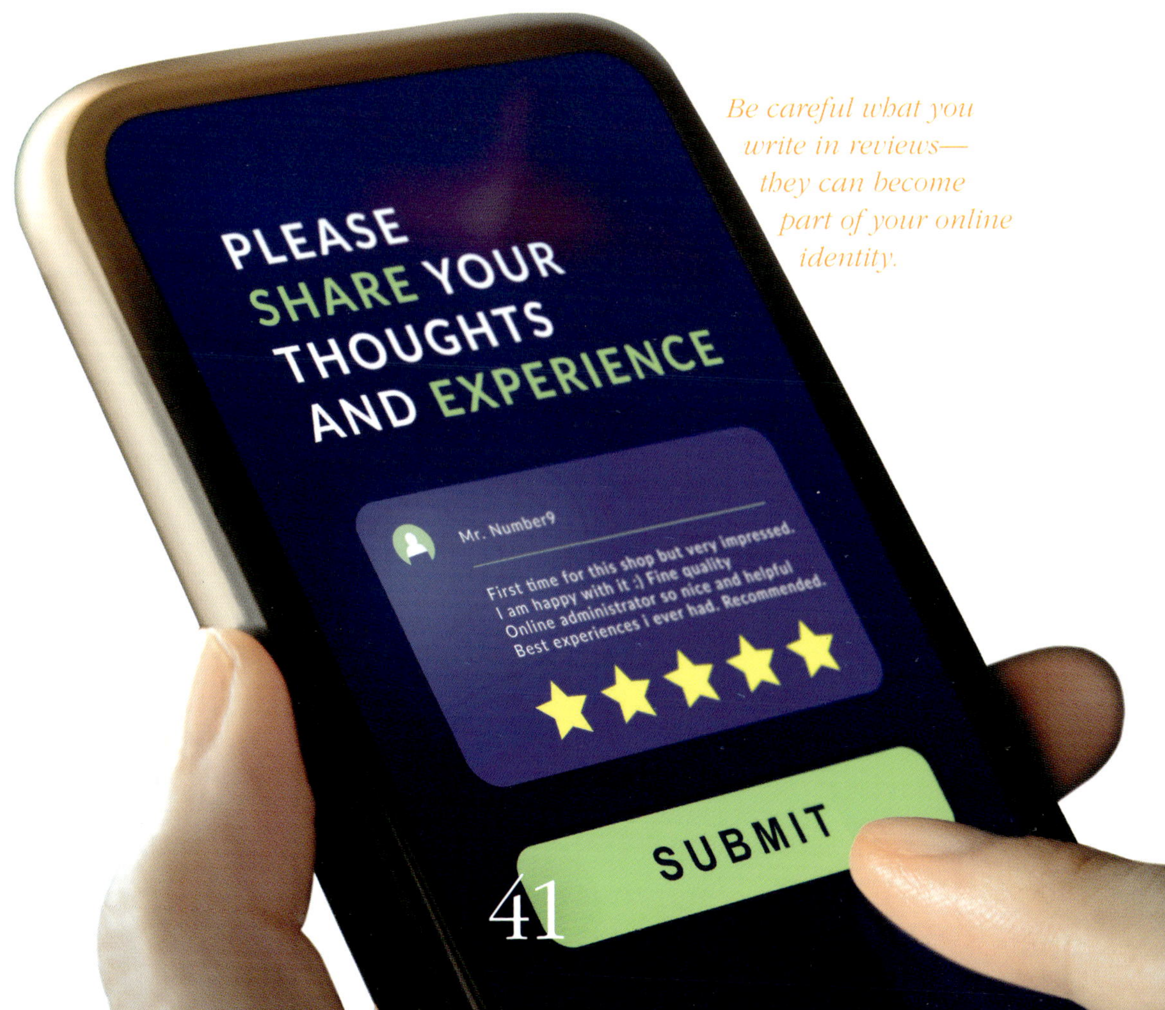

Be careful what you write in reviews—they can become part of your online identity.

CELEBRATE Use the internet to share your accomplishments. You could make a post about winning an award. This helps build a positive online identity. Celebrate your success online. Let trusted friends and family share your joy! Remember to not compare yourself with others. Most people share only positive things. Don't compete. Congratulate them instead.

70 Percent of Americans who have at least one social media account.

Employers often search for applicants' social media profiles. This is called a social media background check. • Double-check before you post. Some sites don't let you go back to fix typos.

Tips for

Use Strong Passwords

Need a good way to think up passwords? Think of a phrase you can easily remember. Use the first letter of each word in the quote to make an acronym. Imagine your phrase is "I want to protect my online privacy forever!" Your acronym could be "Iwtpmop4e!"

Set Up Extra Security

Many sites let you set up "two-factor authentication." This means you must prove your identity twice when logging in. For example, you may enter your password. Then you might enter a code the site sent to your email. This greatly reduces the risk of someone else gaining access to your account.

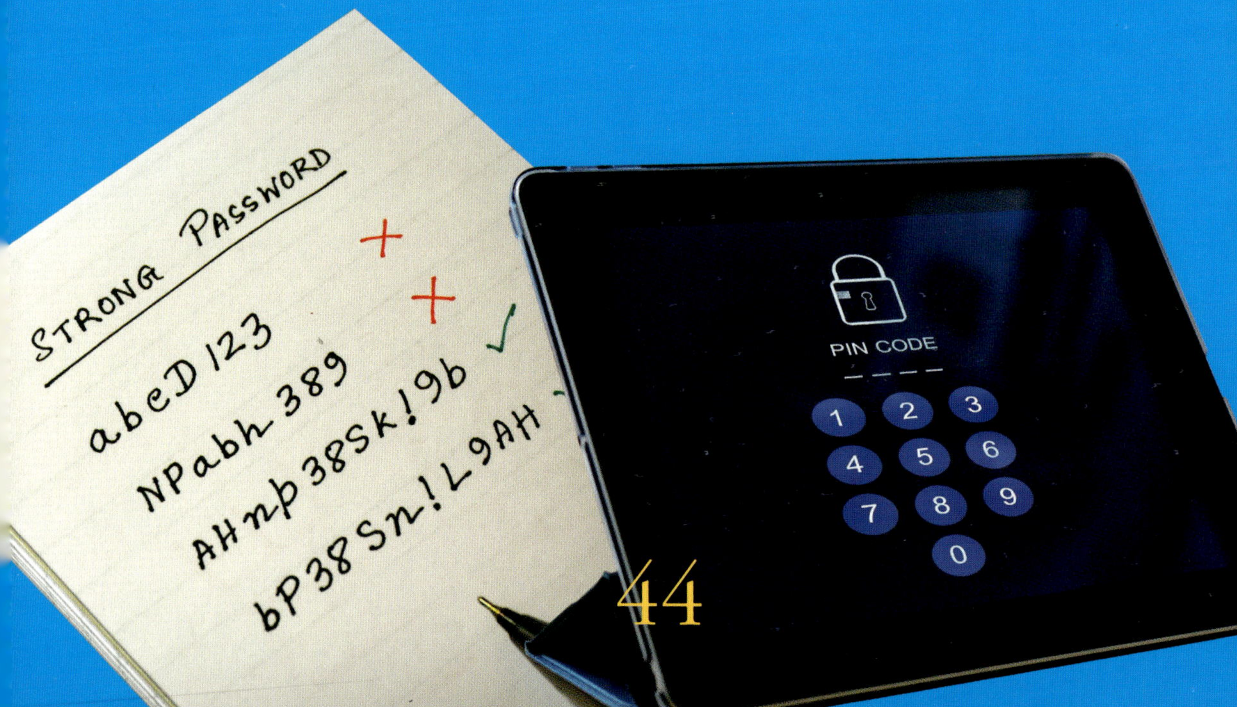

Online Safety

Beware of Fake Accounts

Strangers could pretend to be someone you know. This is called "catfishing." They might use a relative's photos and name to make an account. They could then befriend you. Once they do, they could ask for private information. Be suspicious of new accounts. Do they have any posts? If not, it is likely a scammer.

Flag Content

There may be a time when someone shares your private information online. Most social media sites let you report comments and posts. This is called flagging. It can help your private information stay private.

Glossary

browse
To use an internet browser to find and look at information.

character
A symbol that is used in writing or printing.

data
Information created or stored by a computer.

identity
Who someone is.

identity theft
The illegal use of someone else's private information in order to get money or credit.

monitor
To watch, observe, or check something over a period of time.

offensive
Causing someone to feel hurt, angry, or upset.

partial
Not complete or total.

persona
The way you behave and talk with other people that causes them to see you as a particular kind of person.

predator
A person who looks for other people in order to use, control, or harm them in some way.

preference
A feeling of liking or wanting one person or thing more than another person or thing.

regulate
To bring something under the control of authority.

secure
Protected from danger or harm.

spyware
Software that secretly records information about the way you use your device.

For More Information

Books

Carser, A. R. *Protect Your Data and Identity Online.* San Diego, CA: BrightPoint Press, 2022.

Freedman, Jeri. *Privacy, Data Harvesting, and You.* New York: Rosen Publishing, 2020.

Kim, Carol. *Are Smartphones a Threat to Privacy?* San Diego, CA: ReferencePoint Press, 2021.

Websites

How Secure Is My Password?
www.security.org/how-secure-is-my-password/

NOVA Cybersecurity Lab Game
www.pbs.org/wgbh/nova/labs/lab/cyber/

Online Safety
kidshealth.org/en/kids/online-id.html

About the Author

Marysa Storm is an author and editor who has worked on subjects ranging from pets and wildlife, to yoga and ceremonial magic. She lives in the Twin Cities area with her better half and their tortoiseshell cat. She spends her free time reading tarot, working on sewing projects, and rewatching *The X-Files.*

Index

TOP RANK is published by Black Rabbit Books, P.O. Box 227, Mankato, MN, 56002. • • Designed by Danny Nanos • Photographs © Dreamstime/Adonis1969, 18, Daniel Gilbey, cover, 1, 5, Winterling, 15; Shutterstock/alexskopje, 13, Anatoliy Karlyuk, 20, andras_csontos, 14, 16, Andrey_Kuzmin, 6, Andrey_Popov, 34–35, andy0man, 10, Belinda Pretorius, 48, Bits And Splits, 26, Black Salmon, 41, Brian A Jackson, 32–33, Creative Lab, 45, Dmitry Demidovich, 33, Eviart, 2–3, 27, Feng Yu, 31, giggsy25, 44, Inkoly, 37, Jne Valokuvaus, 17, Jolygon, 46–47, Joseph Sohm, 42–43, Kaspars Grinvalds, 18–19, Kotin, 4, 7, larry1235, 12, Linaimages, 23, 44, Little Vignettes Photo, 8–9, Live2Create, 30, Marcos Mesa Sam Wordley, 45, Mdisk, 38–39, New Africa, 2, 11, 28–29, nito, 24, Romas_Photo, 25, Studio Romantic, 40, Summit Art Creations, 21, TimeStopper69, 22, Trifonenkolvan, 36 • Printed in India
Library of Congress Cataloging-in-Publication Data: Names: Storm, Marysa, author. | Title: 12 questions about online identity and privacy / by Marysa Storm. | Other titles: Twelve questions about online identity and privacy | Description: Mankato, MN: Top Rank, an imprint of Black Rabbit Books, [2026] | Series: Tech smarts | Includes bibliographical references and index. | Ages 9–13 | Grades 4–6 | Identifiers: LCCN 2024054650 (print) | LCCN 2024054651 (ebook) | ISBN 9781644668184 (library binding) | ISBN 9781644668504 (paperback) | ISBN 9781644668825 (ebook) | Subjects: LCSH: Online identities—Juvenile literature. | Internet and children—Juvenile literature. | Internet—Safety measures—Juvenile literature. | Privacy—Juvenile literature. | Privacy, Right of—Juvenile literature. | Classification: LCC HQ784.I58 S76 2026 (print) | LCC HQ784.I58 (ebook) | DDC 302.3—dc23/eng/20241221 | LC record available at https://lccn.loc.gov/2024054650